50 Healthy Air Fryer Favorite Recipes for Home

By: Kelly Johnson

Table of Contents

- Crispy Air Fryer Buffalo Cauliflower
- Air Fryer Baked Apples
- Air Fryer Lemon Garlic Shrimp
- Air Fryer Sweet Potato Fries
- Air Fryer Turkey Meatballs
- Air Fryer Teriyaki Chicken
- Air Fryer Coconut Shrimp
- Air Fryer Chicken Parmesan
- Air Fryer Roasted Brussels Sprouts
- Air Fryer Falafel
- Air Fryer Veggie Chips (carrots, zucchini, sweet potatoes)
- Air Fryer Fish Tacos
- Air Fryer Lemon Pepper Chicken Wings
- Air Fryer Avocado Fries
- Air Fryer Greek Chicken Souvlaki
- Air Fryer Cauliflower Tacos
- Air Fryer Garlic Parmesan Wings
- Air Fryer Zucchini Fritters
- Air Fryer Salmon Cakes
- Air Fryer Honey Garlic Chicken
- Air Fryer Stuffed Peppers
- Air Fryer Coconut-Crusted Chicken Tenders
- Air Fryer Balsamic Brussels Sprouts
- Air Fryer Tofu Nuggets
- Air Fryer Roasted Garlic Potatoes
- Air Fryer Chicken Satay Skewers
- Air Fryer Kale Chips
- Air Fryer Orange Chicken
- Air Fryer Ratatouille
- Air Fryer Chicken Fajitas
- Air Fryer Butternut Squash Fries
- Air Fryer Korean BBQ Wings
- Air Fryer Quinoa-Stuffed Bell Peppers
- Air Fryer Veggie Spring Rolls
- Air Fryer Parmesan Crusted Asparagus

- Air Fryer Jamaican Jerk Chicken
- Air Fryer Stuffed Mushrooms
- Air Fryer Lemon Herb Tofu
- Air Fryer Green Bean Fries
- Air Fryer Cajun Shrimp
- Air Fryer Stuffed Zucchini Boats
- Air Fryer Greek Veggie Patties
- Air Fryer Cinnamon Apple Chips
- Air Fryer Chicken Shawarma
- Air Fryer Mexican Street Corn
- Air Fryer Spicy Cauliflower Bites
- Air Fryer Caprese Stuffed Chicken
- Air Fryer Curried Chickpeas
- Air Fryer Chili-Lime Chicken Drumsticks
- Air Fryer Mediterranean Veggie Skewers

Crispy Air Fryer Buffalo Cauliflower

Ingredients:

- 1 medium head cauliflower, cut into florets
- 1/2 cup all-purpose flour (or chickpea flour for a gluten-free option)
- 1/2 cup water
- 1 teaspoon garlic powder
- 1 teaspoon onion powder
- Salt and pepper to taste
- 1/2 cup buffalo sauce
- Cooking spray

Instructions:

1. Preheat the Air Fryer: Preheat your air fryer to 375°F (190°C) for 5 minutes.
2. Prepare the Batter: In a mixing bowl, whisk together the flour, water, garlic powder, onion powder, salt, and pepper until smooth and well combined.
3. Coat the Cauliflower: Dip each cauliflower floret into the batter, ensuring it's evenly coated. Shake off any excess batter.
4. Air Fry the Cauliflower: Lightly coat the air fryer basket with cooking spray. Place the battered cauliflower florets in a single layer in the air fryer basket, making sure they're not touching each other. You may need to fry them in batches depending on the size of your air fryer. Spray the cauliflower with cooking spray.
5. Cook: Air fry the cauliflower at 375°F (190°C) for 15-20 minutes, flipping halfway through, or until they are golden brown and crispy.
6. Toss in Buffalo Sauce: Once the cauliflower is cooked, transfer it to a mixing bowl and toss it with buffalo sauce until evenly coated.
7. Serve: Serve the crispy buffalo cauliflower immediately as a delicious appetizer or snack. You can garnish with chopped fresh cilantro or parsley if desired.

Enjoy the spicy and crispy goodness of these air-fried buffalo cauliflower bites, perfect for game day or any gathering!

Air Fryer Baked Apples

Ingredients:

- 4 medium-sized apples (such as Granny Smith or Honeycrisp)
- 2 tablespoons melted butter or coconut oil
- 2 tablespoons brown sugar or coconut sugar
- 1 teaspoon ground cinnamon
- 1/4 teaspoon ground nutmeg
- 1/4 cup chopped nuts (such as walnuts or pecans), optional
- Vanilla ice cream or whipped cream, for serving (optional)

Instructions:

1. Preheat the Air Fryer: Preheat your air fryer to 375°F (190°C) for 5 minutes.
2. Prepare the Apples: Wash the apples and pat them dry. Core each apple using an apple corer or a knife, making sure to leave the bottom intact to create a well for the filling.
3. Make the Filling: In a small bowl, mix together the melted butter or coconut oil, brown sugar or coconut sugar, ground cinnamon, and ground nutmeg until well combined. If using chopped nuts, add them to the filling mixture and mix until evenly distributed.
4. Fill the Apples: Spoon the filling mixture into the well of each cored apple, distributing it evenly among them.
5. Air Fry the Apples: Place the filled apples in the air fryer basket or tray, making sure they are not touching each other. Air fry at 375°F (190°C) for 15-20 minutes, or until the apples are tender and the filling is bubbling and caramelized.
6. Serve: Remove the baked apples from the air fryer and let them cool slightly before serving. Serve them warm with a scoop of vanilla ice cream or a dollop of whipped cream, if desired.
7. Enjoy: Enjoy these delicious air fryer baked apples as a healthier dessert option that's perfect for any occasion!

These air fryer baked apples are tender, sweet, and filled with warm spices, making them a comforting treat that's sure to please.

Air Fryer Lemon Garlic Shrimp

Ingredients:

- 1 lb large shrimp, peeled and deveined
- 2 tablespoons olive oil
- 3 cloves garlic, minced
- Zest of 1 lemon
- Juice of 1 lemon
- 1 teaspoon dried Italian seasoning (or a mix of dried oregano, basil, and thyme)
- Salt and pepper, to taste
- Chopped fresh parsley, for garnish
- Lemon wedges, for serving

Instructions:

1. Preheat the Air Fryer: Preheat your air fryer to 400°F (200°C) for 5 minutes.
2. Prepare the Shrimp: In a mixing bowl, combine the peeled and deveined shrimp with olive oil, minced garlic, lemon zest, lemon juice, dried Italian seasoning, salt, and pepper. Toss until the shrimp are evenly coated with the marinade.
3. Cook the Shrimp: Once the air fryer is preheated, place the seasoned shrimp in the air fryer basket in a single layer, making sure they are not overcrowded. Cook in batches if necessary.
4. Air Fry: Air fry the shrimp at 400°F (200°C) for 5-7 minutes, flipping halfway through, or until they are pink and opaque.
5. Serve: Once cooked, transfer the lemon garlic shrimp to a serving platter. Garnish with chopped fresh parsley and serve immediately with lemon wedges on the side for squeezing.
6. Enjoy: Enjoy these flavorful air fryer lemon garlic shrimp as a main dish with a side of rice or pasta, or serve them as a delicious appetizer for your next gathering.

These air-fried shrimp are tender, juicy, and infused with the bright flavors of lemon and garlic, making them a tasty and satisfying dish that's sure to impress!

Air Fryer Sweet Potato Fries

Ingredients:

- 2 large sweet potatoes, peeled and cut into fries
- 2 tablespoons olive oil
- 1 teaspoon paprika
- 1/2 teaspoon garlic powder
- 1/2 teaspoon onion powder
- 1/2 teaspoon salt, or to taste
- 1/4 teaspoon black pepper

Instructions:

1. Preheat the Air Fryer: Preheat your air fryer to 380°F (190°C) for 5 minutes.
2. Prepare the Sweet Potatoes: In a large bowl, toss the sweet potato fries with olive oil until evenly coated.
3. Season the Fries: Add paprika, garlic powder, onion powder, salt, and black pepper to the bowl with the sweet potatoes. Toss until the fries are evenly coated with the seasonings.
4. Air Fry the Fries: Place the seasoned sweet potato fries in the air fryer basket in a single layer, making sure they are not overcrowded. Cook in batches if necessary.
5. Air Fry: Air fry the sweet potato fries at 380°F (190°C) for 15-20 minutes, shaking the basket halfway through the cooking time, until the fries are crispy and golden brown.
6. Serve: Once cooked, transfer the sweet potato fries to a serving platter and serve immediately.
7. Optional: Serve with your favorite dipping sauce, such as ketchup, aioli, or spicy mayo, for added flavor.

Enjoy these crispy and flavorful air fryer sweet potato fries as a delicious side dish or snack that's perfect for any occasion!

Air Fryer Turkey Meatballs

Ingredients:

- 1 lb ground turkey
- 1/4 cup breadcrumbs (or almond flour for a gluten-free option)
- 1/4 cup grated Parmesan cheese
- 1 egg, beaten
- 2 cloves garlic, minced
- 1 teaspoon dried oregano
- 1 teaspoon dried basil
- 1/2 teaspoon onion powder
- 1/2 teaspoon salt
- 1/4 teaspoon black pepper
- Cooking spray

Instructions:

1. Preheat the Air Fryer: Preheat your air fryer to 375°F (190°C) for 5 minutes.
2. Mix the Ingredients: In a large mixing bowl, combine the ground turkey, breadcrumbs, Parmesan cheese, beaten egg, minced garlic, dried oregano, dried basil, onion powder, salt, and black pepper. Mix until well combined.
3. Shape the Meatballs: Using your hands, shape the turkey mixture into meatballs of your desired size. Make sure they are evenly shaped for even cooking.
4. Air Fry the Meatballs: Lightly coat the air fryer basket with cooking spray. Place the meatballs in the air fryer basket in a single layer, making sure they are not touching each other. You may need to cook them in batches depending on the size of your air fryer.
5. Cook: Air fry the turkey meatballs at 375°F (190°C) for 12-15 minutes, shaking the basket halfway through the cooking time, until they are golden brown and cooked through. The internal temperature should reach 165°F (74°C).
6. Serve: Once cooked, remove the turkey meatballs from the air fryer and let them cool slightly before serving.
7. Optional: Serve the turkey meatballs with your favorite sauce, such as marinara sauce, barbecue sauce, or pesto, for dipping or drizzling.

Enjoy these delicious and healthy air fryer turkey meatballs as a tasty appetizer, a protein-packed main dish, or as part of your favorite pasta dish!

Air Fryer Teriyaki Chicken

Ingredients:

- 1 lb boneless, skinless chicken thighs or breasts, cut into bite-sized pieces
- 1/4 cup soy sauce
- 2 tablespoons honey or maple syrup
- 1 tablespoon rice vinegar
- 1 tablespoon sesame oil
- 2 cloves garlic, minced
- 1 teaspoon grated ginger
- 1 tablespoon cornstarch
- 1 tablespoon water
- Sesame seeds and chopped green onions, for garnish (optional)

Instructions:

1. Marinate the Chicken: In a bowl, combine soy sauce, honey or maple syrup, rice vinegar, sesame oil, minced garlic, and grated ginger. Add the chicken pieces to the bowl and toss to coat evenly. Let the chicken marinate for at least 30 minutes in the refrigerator.
2. Preheat the Air Fryer: Preheat your air fryer to 380°F (190°C) for 5 minutes.
3. Prepare the Sauce: In a small bowl, mix cornstarch with water to make a slurry. Set aside. Transfer the marinated chicken and sauce to a cooking-safe dish that fits inside your air fryer basket.
4. Air Fry the Chicken: Place the dish with the marinated chicken in the air fryer basket. Cook at 380°F (190°C) for 15-18 minutes, shaking the basket halfway through the cooking time. The chicken should be golden brown and cooked through.
5. Thicken the Sauce: Once the chicken is cooked, remove the dish from the air fryer. Pour the cooking liquid into a small saucepan. Bring it to a simmer over medium heat. Stir in the cornstarch slurry and cook for 1-2 minutes, stirring constantly, until the sauce thickens.
6. Serve: Pour the thickened teriyaki sauce over the cooked chicken. Garnish with sesame seeds and chopped green onions, if desired. Serve hot with rice or vegetables.

Enjoy this delicious Air Fryer Teriyaki Chicken as a quick and easy weeknight meal or as part of a tasty Asian-inspired dinner!

Air Fryer Coconut Shrimp

Ingredients:

- 1 lb large shrimp, peeled and deveined
- 1/2 cup all-purpose flour
- 2 large eggs, beaten
- 1 cup shredded coconut (unsweetened)
- 1/2 cup panko breadcrumbs
- 1/2 teaspoon salt
- 1/4 teaspoon black pepper
- Cooking spray

Instructions:

1. Preheat the Air Fryer: Preheat your air fryer to 400°F (200°C) for 5 minutes.
2. Prepare the Breading Station: Set up a breading station with three shallow bowls. In one bowl, place the all-purpose flour. In the second bowl, beat the eggs. In the third bowl, combine shredded coconut, panko breadcrumbs, salt, and black pepper.
3. Bread the Shrimp: Take each shrimp and dredge it first in the flour, then dip it into the beaten eggs, and finally coat it thoroughly with the coconut-panko mixture. Press gently to adhere the breading to the shrimp. Place the breaded shrimp on a plate or baking sheet.
4. Arrange the Shrimp in the Air Fryer: Lightly coat the air fryer basket with cooking spray. Place the breaded shrimp in a single layer in the air fryer basket, making sure they are not touching each other. You may need to cook them in batches depending on the size of your air fryer.
5. Air Fry the Shrimp: Air fry the coconut shrimp at 400°F (200°C) for 6-8 minutes, flipping halfway through the cooking time, until they are golden brown and crispy.
6. Serve: Once cooked, remove the coconut shrimp from the air fryer and let them cool slightly before serving. Serve them with your favorite dipping sauce, such as sweet chili sauce or mango salsa.

Enjoy these crispy and flavorful Air Fryer Coconut Shrimp as an appetizer or as part of a main course. They're sure to be a hit at your next gathering or dinner party!

Air Fryer Chicken Parmesan

Ingredients:

- 4 boneless, skinless chicken breasts
- 1 cup breadcrumbs (panko or Italian-style)
- 1/2 cup grated Parmesan cheese
- 1 teaspoon dried Italian seasoning
- 1/2 teaspoon garlic powder
- 1/2 teaspoon onion powder
- Salt and pepper, to taste
- 2 eggs, beaten
- 1 cup marinara sauce
- 1 cup shredded mozzarella cheese
- Cooking spray
- Fresh basil leaves, for garnish (optional)

Instructions:

1. Preheat the Air Fryer: Preheat your air fryer to 380°F (190°C) for 5 minutes.
2. Prepare the Chicken: Place each chicken breast between two sheets of plastic wrap or parchment paper. Use a meat mallet or rolling pin to pound the chicken to an even thickness of about 1/2 inch. Season the chicken breasts with salt and pepper on both sides.
3. Prepare the Breading Station: In a shallow dish, combine breadcrumbs, grated Parmesan cheese, dried Italian seasoning, garlic powder, and onion powder. In another shallow dish, place the beaten eggs.
4. Bread the Chicken: Dip each seasoned chicken breast into the beaten eggs, then coat it evenly with the breadcrumb mixture, pressing gently to adhere. Repeat with the remaining chicken breasts.
5. Air Fry the Chicken: Lightly coat the air fryer basket with cooking spray. Place the breaded chicken breasts in the air fryer basket in a single layer, making sure they are not touching each other. You may need to cook them in batches depending on the size of your air fryer.
6. Cook: Air fry the chicken breasts at 380°F (190°C) for 10-12 minutes, flipping halfway through the cooking time, until they are golden brown and cooked through.
7. Add Sauce and Cheese: Once the chicken is cooked, top each breast with marinara sauce and shredded mozzarella cheese.

8. Finish Cooking: Return the chicken to the air fryer and cook for an additional 2-3 minutes, or until the cheese is melted and bubbly.
9. Serve: Once cooked, remove the chicken Parmesan from the air fryer and let it cool slightly before serving. Garnish with fresh basil leaves, if desired.

Enjoy this delicious and healthier version of Chicken Parmesan, made crispy and flavorful in the air fryer! Serve it with pasta or a side salad for a complete meal.

Air Fryer Roasted Brussels Sprouts

Ingredients:

- 1 lb Brussels sprouts, trimmed and halved
- 2 tablespoons olive oil
- 2 cloves garlic, minced
- 1 teaspoon smoked paprika
- Salt and pepper, to taste
- Grated Parmesan cheese (optional)
- Balsamic glaze (optional)

Instructions:

1. Preheat the Air Fryer: Preheat your air fryer to 375°F (190°C) for 5 minutes.
2. Prepare the Brussels Sprouts: In a large bowl, toss the Brussels sprouts with olive oil, minced garlic, smoked paprika, salt, and pepper until evenly coated.
3. Air Fry the Brussels Sprouts: Place the seasoned Brussels sprouts in the air fryer basket in a single layer, making sure they are not overcrowded. You may need to cook them in batches depending on the size of your air fryer.
4. Cook: Air fry the Brussels sprouts at 375°F (190°C) for 12-15 minutes, shaking the basket halfway through the cooking time, until they are crispy and browned on the edges.
5. Serve: Once cooked, transfer the roasted Brussels sprouts to a serving dish. If desired, sprinkle with grated Parmesan cheese and drizzle with balsamic glaze for extra flavor.
6. Enjoy: Serve the air fryer roasted Brussels sprouts immediately as a delicious and nutritious side dish to accompany any meal.

These air fryer roasted Brussels sprouts are crispy, flavorful, and incredibly easy to make. They're sure to become a favorite addition to your dinner table!

Air Fryer Falafel

Ingredients:

- 1 cup dried chickpeas, soaked overnight (or 1 can of chickpeas, drained and rinsed)
- 1 small onion, chopped
- 3 cloves garlic, minced
- 1/4 cup fresh parsley, chopped
- 1/4 cup fresh cilantro, chopped
- 1 teaspoon ground cumin
- 1 teaspoon ground coriander
- 1/2 teaspoon baking soda
- 1 tablespoon all-purpose flour (or chickpea flour for a gluten-free option)
- Salt and pepper, to taste
- Cooking spray

Instructions:

1. Preheat the Air Fryer: Preheat your air fryer to 375°F (190°C) for 5 minutes.
2. Prepare the Falafel Mixture: In a food processor, combine the soaked chickpeas, chopped onion, minced garlic, chopped parsley, chopped cilantro, ground cumin, ground coriander, baking soda, flour, salt, and pepper. Pulse until the mixture is coarsely ground and holds together when pressed.
3. Form the Falafel: Scoop out tablespoon-sized portions of the falafel mixture and shape them into balls or patties. Place them on a plate or baking sheet lined with parchment paper.
4. Air Fry the Falafel: Lightly coat the air fryer basket with cooking spray. Place the formed falafel in the air fryer basket in a single layer, making sure they are not touching each other. You may need to cook them in batches depending on the size of your air fryer.
5. Cook: Air fry the falafel at 375°F (190°C) for 10-12 minutes, flipping halfway through the cooking time, until they are golden brown and crispy on the outside.
6. Serve: Once cooked, remove the falafel from the air fryer and let them cool slightly before serving. Serve them with your favorite toppings and sauces, such as tahini sauce, tzatziki, or hummus.
7. Enjoy: Enjoy these delicious and healthier air fryer falafel as a tasty appetizer, snack, or part of a Mediterranean-inspired meal!

These air-fried falafel are crispy on the outside, soft and flavorful on the inside, and perfect for satisfying your falafel cravings without the need for deep frying.

Air Fryer Veggie Chips (carrots, zucchini, sweet potatoes)

Ingredients:

- 1 large carrot, peeled
- 1 medium zucchini
- 1 small sweet potato, peeled
- 1-2 tablespoons olive oil
- Salt and pepper, to taste
- Optional seasonings: garlic powder, paprika, Italian seasoning, etc.

Instructions:

1. Preheat the Air Fryer: Preheat your air fryer to 375°F (190°C) for 5 minutes.
2. Prepare the Vegetables: Using a mandoline slicer or a sharp knife, thinly slice the carrot, zucchini, and sweet potato into rounds. Try to make the slices as uniform in thickness as possible for even cooking.
3. Season the Vegetables: In a large bowl, toss the sliced vegetables with olive oil until evenly coated. Season with salt, pepper, and any additional seasonings of your choice, such as garlic powder, paprika, or Italian seasoning.
4. Arrange in the Air Fryer: Arrange the seasoned vegetable slices in a single layer in the air fryer basket, making sure they are not overlapping. You may need to cook them in batches depending on the size of your air fryer.
5. Air Fry: Air fry the veggie chips at 375°F (190°C) for 8-10 minutes, flipping halfway through the cooking time, until they are crispy and golden brown.
6. Serve: Once cooked, remove the veggie chips from the air fryer and let them cool slightly before serving. Serve them as a healthy snack or side dish with your favorite dipping sauce, such as hummus or tzatziki.
7. Enjoy: Enjoy these crispy and flavorful air fryer veggie chips as a nutritious alternative to store-bought chips. Experiment with different vegetables and seasonings to create your own customized chip blend!

These air-fried veggie chips are crunchy, satisfying, and packed with vitamins and minerals, making them a guilt-free snack option for any occasion.

Air Fryer Fish Tacos

Ingredients:

- 1 lb white fish fillets (such as cod, tilapia, or halibut)
- 1 cup all-purpose flour (or cornmeal for a gluten-free option)
- 2 eggs, beaten
- 1 cup panko breadcrumbs
- 1 teaspoon chili powder
- 1/2 teaspoon garlic powder
- 1/2 teaspoon paprika
- Salt and pepper, to taste
- Cooking spray
- Corn or flour tortillas
- Shredded cabbage or lettuce
- Sliced avocado
- Salsa or pico de gallo
- Lime wedges, for serving
- Optional toppings: sour cream, cilantro, jalapeños

Instructions:

1. Preheat the Air Fryer: Preheat your air fryer to 400°F (200°C) for 5 minutes.
2. Prepare the Fish: Cut the fish fillets into strips or bite-sized pieces. Season the fish with salt and pepper.
3. Set Up the Breading Station: In three separate shallow bowls, place the flour in the first bowl, beaten eggs in the second bowl, and panko breadcrumbs mixed with chili powder, garlic powder, and paprika in the third bowl.
4. Bread the Fish: Dredge each piece of seasoned fish in the flour, then dip it into the beaten eggs, and finally coat it with the seasoned panko breadcrumbs, pressing gently to adhere. Repeat with the remaining fish pieces.
5. Air Fry the Fish: Lightly coat the air fryer basket with cooking spray. Arrange the breaded fish pieces in a single layer in the air fryer basket, making sure they are not overlapping. You may need to cook them in batches depending on the size of your air fryer.
6. Air Fry: Air fry the fish at 400°F (200°C) for 8-10 minutes, flipping halfway through the cooking time, until the fish is golden brown and cooked through.

7. Assemble the Tacos: Warm the tortillas in the air fryer or microwave. Fill each tortilla with shredded cabbage or lettuce, sliced avocado, air-fried fish, and your choice of salsa or pico de gallo.
8. Serve: Serve the fish tacos immediately with lime wedges on the side for squeezing. Garnish with optional toppings such as sour cream, cilantro, or jalapeños.
9. Enjoy: Enjoy these delicious and healthier air fryer fish tacos as a satisfying meal that's perfect for lunch or dinner!

These air-fried fish tacos are crispy, flavorful, and packed with fresh ingredients, making them a crowd-pleasing dish that's sure to impress!

Air Fryer Lemon Pepper Chicken Wings

Ingredients:

- 2 lbs chicken wings, split into flats and drumettes
- 2 tablespoons olive oil
- Zest of 1 lemon
- Juice of 1 lemon
- 1 teaspoon lemon pepper seasoning
- 1/2 teaspoon garlic powder
- 1/2 teaspoon onion powder
- Salt and pepper, to taste
- Cooking spray

Instructions:

1. Preheat the Air Fryer: Preheat your air fryer to 380°F (190°C) for 5 minutes.
2. Prepare the Chicken Wings: Pat the chicken wings dry with paper towels to remove excess moisture. Place them in a large bowl.
3. Season the Wings: Drizzle the olive oil over the chicken wings and toss to coat evenly. Add the lemon zest, lemon juice, lemon pepper seasoning, garlic powder, onion powder, salt, and pepper. Toss again until the wings are evenly coated with the seasoning mixture.
4. Arrange in the Air Fryer: Lightly coat the air fryer basket with cooking spray. Arrange the seasoned chicken wings in a single layer in the air fryer basket, making sure they are not overcrowded. You may need to cook them in batches depending on the size of your air fryer.
5. Air Fry the Wings: Air fry the chicken wings at 380°F (190°C) for 25-30 minutes, flipping halfway through the cooking time, until they are golden brown and crispy. The internal temperature of the wings should reach 165°F (74°C).
6. Serve: Once cooked, transfer the lemon pepper chicken wings to a serving platter. Garnish with additional lemon zest and freshly cracked black pepper if desired. Serve them hot with your favorite dipping sauce, such as ranch dressing or blue cheese dressing.
7. Enjoy: Enjoy these delicious air fryer lemon pepper chicken wings as a flavorful appetizer or main dish, perfect for game day or any gathering!

These air-fried chicken wings are crispy on the outside, tender and juicy on the inside, and bursting with zesty lemon pepper flavor. They're sure to be a hit with family and friends!

Air Fryer Avocado Fries

Ingredients:

- 2 ripe avocados
- 1/2 cup all-purpose flour
- 2 eggs, beaten
- 1 cup panko breadcrumbs
- 1/4 cup grated Parmesan cheese
- 1/2 teaspoon garlic powder
- 1/2 teaspoon paprika
- 1/2 teaspoon salt
- 1/4 teaspoon black pepper
- Cooking spray

Instructions:

1. Preheat the Air Fryer: Preheat your air fryer to 400°F (200°C) for 5 minutes.
2. Prepare the Avocados: Cut the avocados in half, remove the pits, and slice each half into thick wedges. Carefully scoop out the avocado wedges with a spoon.
3. Set Up the Breading Station: In three separate shallow bowls, place the all-purpose flour in the first bowl, beaten eggs in the second bowl, and panko breadcrumbs mixed with grated Parmesan cheese, garlic powder, paprika, salt, and black pepper in the third bowl.
4. Bread the Avocado Wedges: Dredge each avocado wedge in the flour, then dip it into the beaten eggs, and finally coat it with the seasoned panko breadcrumb mixture, pressing gently to adhere. Repeat with the remaining avocado wedges.
5. Air Fry the Avocado Fries: Lightly coat the air fryer basket with cooking spray. Arrange the breaded avocado wedges in a single layer in the air fryer basket, making sure they are not overlapping. You may need to cook them in batches depending on the size of your air fryer.
6. Air Fry: Air fry the avocado fries at 400°F (200°C) for 8-10 minutes, flipping halfway through the cooking time, until they are golden brown and crispy.
7. Serve: Once cooked, remove the avocado fries from the air fryer and let them cool slightly before serving. Serve them with your favorite dipping sauce, such as sriracha mayo, chipotle aioli, or ranch dressing.
8. Enjoy: Enjoy these crispy and creamy air fryer avocado fries as a tasty appetizer or snack that's sure to impress!

These air-fried avocado fries are a delicious and healthier alternative to traditional fries, perfect for any occasion. They're crispy on the outside, creamy on the inside, and bursting with flavor!

Air Fryer Greek Chicken Souvlaki

Ingredients:

- 1 lb chicken breast, cut into bite-sized pieces
- 2 tablespoons olive oil
- 2 tablespoons lemon juice
- 2 cloves garlic, minced
- 1 teaspoon dried oregano
- 1/2 teaspoon dried thyme
- 1/2 teaspoon paprika
- Salt and pepper, to taste
- Tzatziki sauce, for serving
- Pita bread, for serving
- Sliced cucumbers, tomatoes, onions, and lettuce, for serving

Instructions:

1. Marinate the Chicken: In a bowl, combine the olive oil, lemon juice, minced garlic, dried oregano, dried thyme, paprika, salt, and pepper. Add the chicken pieces to the marinade and toss until well coated. Cover the bowl and let the chicken marinate in the refrigerator for at least 30 minutes, or overnight for best results.
2. Preheat the Air Fryer: Preheat your air fryer to 400°F (200°C) for 5 minutes.
3. Skewer the Chicken: Thread the marinated chicken pieces onto skewers, leaving a little space between each piece.
4. Air Fry the Chicken: Lightly coat the air fryer basket with cooking spray. Place the chicken skewers in the air fryer basket in a single layer, making sure they are not touching each other. You may need to cook them in batches depending on the size of your air fryer.
5. Air Fry: Air fry the chicken skewers at 400°F (200°C) for 10-12 minutes, flipping halfway through the cooking time, until the chicken is cooked through and golden brown on the outside.
6. Serve: Once cooked, remove the chicken skewers from the air fryer and let them rest for a few minutes. Serve the Greek chicken souvlaki with tzatziki sauce, pita bread, and your choice of sliced cucumbers, tomatoes, onions, and lettuce.
7. Enjoy: Enjoy these delicious Greek chicken souvlaki skewers as a flavorful and satisfying meal that's perfect for any occasion!

These air-fried Greek chicken souvlaki skewers are tender, juicy, and packed with Mediterranean flavors. They're sure to be a hit with family and friends!

Air Fryer Cauliflower Tacos

Ingredients:

- 1 head cauliflower, cut into florets
- 2 tablespoons olive oil
- 1 teaspoon chili powder
- 1 teaspoon cumin
- 1/2 teaspoon smoked paprika
- 1/2 teaspoon garlic powder
- 1/2 teaspoon onion powder
- Salt and pepper, to taste
- Corn or flour tortillas
- Toppings: shredded cabbage or lettuce, diced tomatoes, avocado slices, chopped cilantro, lime wedges, etc.
- Optional: salsa, sour cream, hot sauce, or your favorite taco sauce

Instructions:

1. Preheat the Air Fryer: Preheat your air fryer to 375°F (190°C) for 5 minutes.
2. Prepare the Cauliflower: In a large bowl, toss the cauliflower florets with olive oil until evenly coated.
3. Season the Cauliflower: Add chili powder, cumin, smoked paprika, garlic powder, onion powder, salt, and pepper to the bowl with the cauliflower. Toss until the cauliflower is evenly coated with the seasoning mixture.
4. Air Fry the Cauliflower: Lightly coat the air fryer basket with cooking spray. Place the seasoned cauliflower florets in the air fryer basket in a single layer, making sure they are not overcrowded. You may need to cook them in batches depending on the size of your air fryer.
5. Air Fry: Air fry the cauliflower at 375°F (190°C) for 15-20 minutes, shaking the basket halfway through the cooking time, until the cauliflower is tender and golden brown.
6. Warm the Tortillas: While the cauliflower is cooking, warm the tortillas in the air fryer or microwave.
7. Assemble the Tacos: Fill each tortilla with a generous amount of air-fried cauliflower. Top with shredded cabbage or lettuce, diced tomatoes, avocado slices, chopped cilantro, and any other desired toppings.

8. Serve: Serve the cauliflower tacos immediately with lime wedges on the side for squeezing. Drizzle with salsa, sour cream, hot sauce, or your favorite taco sauce, if desired.
9. Enjoy: Enjoy these delicious and flavorful air fryer cauliflower tacos as a tasty vegetarian meal that's perfect for Taco Tuesday or any day of the week!

These air-fried cauliflower tacos are crispy, spicy, and bursting with flavor. They're sure to be a hit with vegetarians and meat-eaters alike!

Air Fryer Garlic Parmesan Wings

Ingredients:

- 2 lbs chicken wings, split into flats and drumettes
- 2 tablespoons olive oil
- 4 cloves garlic, minced
- 1/4 cup grated Parmesan cheese
- 1 teaspoon dried parsley
- 1/2 teaspoon garlic powder
- 1/2 teaspoon onion powder
- Salt and pepper, to taste
- Cooking spray

Instructions:

1. Preheat the Air Fryer: Preheat your air fryer to 400°F (200°C) for 5 minutes.
2. Prepare the Chicken Wings: Pat the chicken wings dry with paper towels to remove excess moisture. Place them in a large bowl.
3. Make the Garlic Parmesan Coating: In a small bowl, combine the minced garlic, grated Parmesan cheese, dried parsley, garlic powder, onion powder, salt, and pepper. Stir in the olive oil to create a paste.
4. Coat the Wings: Add the garlic Parmesan mixture to the bowl with the chicken wings. Toss until the wings are evenly coated with the mixture.
5. Arrange in the Air Fryer: Lightly coat the air fryer basket with cooking spray. Arrange the coated chicken wings in a single layer in the air fryer basket, making sure they are not overlapping. You may need to cook them in batches depending on the size of your air fryer.
6. Air Fry the Wings: Air fry the chicken wings at 400°F (200°C) for 25-30 minutes, flipping halfway through the cooking time, until they are golden brown and crispy.
7. Serve: Once cooked, remove the garlic Parmesan wings from the air fryer and let them cool slightly before serving. Serve them hot with your favorite dipping sauce, such as ranch dressing or blue cheese dressing.
8. Enjoy: Enjoy these delicious air fryer garlic Parmesan wings as a flavorful appetizer or snack that's sure to impress!

These air-fried garlic Parmesan wings are crispy on the outside, tender and juicy on the inside, and packed with savory garlic and Parmesan flavor. They're sure to be a hit at your next party or gathering!

Air Fryer Zucchini Fritters

Ingredients:

- 2 medium zucchinis, grated
- 1 teaspoon salt
- 1/4 cup all-purpose flour (or almond flour for a gluten-free option)
- 1/4 cup grated Parmesan cheese
- 1/4 cup chopped fresh herbs (such as parsley, dill, or basil)
- 2 cloves garlic, minced
- 1/4 teaspoon black pepper
- 2 eggs, beaten
- Cooking spray

Instructions:

1. Prepare the Zucchini: Place the grated zucchini in a colander set over a bowl. Sprinkle with salt and let sit for 10-15 minutes to allow excess moisture to drain.
2. Squeeze Out Excess Moisture: After 10-15 minutes, use your hands or a clean kitchen towel to squeeze out as much liquid from the zucchini as possible.
3. Mix Ingredients: In a large bowl, combine the drained zucchini, flour, grated Parmesan cheese, chopped herbs, minced garlic, black pepper, and beaten eggs. Mix until well combined.
4. Form Fritters: Lightly coat the air fryer basket with cooking spray. Scoop about 1/4 cup of the zucchini mixture and shape it into a fritter. Place the fritter in the air fryer basket. Repeat with the remaining mixture, leaving a little space between each fritter.
5. Air Fry: Air fry the zucchini fritters at 375°F (190°C) for 10-12 minutes, flipping halfway through the cooking time, until they are golden brown and crispy on the outside.
6. Serve: Once cooked, remove the zucchini fritters from the air fryer and let them cool slightly before serving. Serve them with your favorite dipping sauce, such as tzatziki, sour cream, or marinara sauce.
7. Enjoy: Enjoy these delicious air fryer zucchini fritters as a tasty and nutritious snack or side dish!

These air-fried zucchini fritters are crispy on the outside, soft and tender on the inside, and packed with flavor from the fresh herbs and Parmesan cheese. They're sure to be a hit with family and friends!

Air Fryer Salmon Cakes

Ingredients:

- 1 lb salmon fillets, cooked and flaked
- 1/2 cup breadcrumbs (panko or regular)
- 1/4 cup mayonnaise
- 1/4 cup diced red bell pepper
- 2 tablespoons chopped fresh parsley
- 2 green onions, thinly sliced
- 1 tablespoon Dijon mustard
- 1 tablespoon lemon juice
- 1 teaspoon Old Bay seasoning
- Salt and pepper, to taste
- Cooking spray

Instructions:

1. Prepare the Salmon: Cook the salmon fillets by baking, grilling, or poaching them until they are fully cooked and easily flake with a fork. Let them cool slightly, then flake the salmon into small pieces using a fork.
2. Mix the Ingredients: In a large bowl, combine the flaked salmon, breadcrumbs, mayonnaise, diced red bell pepper, chopped parsley, sliced green onions, Dijon mustard, lemon juice, Old Bay seasoning, salt, and pepper. Mix until well combined.
3. Form the Salmon Cakes: Divide the salmon mixture into equal portions and shape them into patties or cakes, about 1/2 inch thick.
4. Preheat the Air Fryer: Preheat your air fryer to 375°F (190°C) for 5 minutes.
5. Air Fry the Salmon Cakes: Lightly coat the air fryer basket with cooking spray. Place the salmon cakes in the air fryer basket in a single layer, leaving a little space between each cake. You may need to cook them in batches depending on the size of your air fryer.
6. Air Fry: Air fry the salmon cakes at 375°F (190°C) for 10-12 minutes, flipping halfway through the cooking time, until they are golden brown and crispy on the outside.
7. Serve: Once cooked, remove the salmon cakes from the air fryer and let them cool slightly before serving. Serve them with your favorite dipping sauce, such as tartar sauce, remoulade, or aioli, and lemon wedges on the side.

8. Enjoy: Enjoy these delicious air fryer salmon cakes as a nutritious and flavorful seafood dish that's perfect for lunch or dinner!

These air-fried salmon cakes are crispy on the outside, tender and moist on the inside, and packed with savory flavors from the salmon and seasonings. They're sure to be a hit with seafood lovers and a welcome addition to any meal!

Air Fryer Honey Garlic Chicken

Ingredients:

- 1 lb chicken breast or thighs, cut into bite-sized pieces
- 3 tablespoons soy sauce
- 2 tablespoons honey
- 2 cloves garlic, minced
- 1 tablespoon olive oil
- 1 teaspoon sesame oil
- 1 teaspoon cornstarch
- Sesame seeds and chopped green onions for garnish (optional)

Instructions:

1. Marinate the Chicken: In a bowl, combine the soy sauce, honey, minced garlic, olive oil, sesame oil, and cornstarch. Add the chicken pieces to the bowl and toss until they are evenly coated with the marinade. Let the chicken marinate for at least 30 minutes in the refrigerator, or overnight for best results.
2. Preheat the Air Fryer: Preheat your air fryer to 380°F (190°C) for 5 minutes.
3. Air Fry the Chicken: Lightly coat the air fryer basket with cooking spray. Place the marinated chicken pieces in the air fryer basket in a single layer, making sure they are not overcrowded. You may need to cook them in batches depending on the size of your air fryer.
4. Cook: Air fry the chicken at 380°F (190°C) for 12-15 minutes, shaking the basket halfway through the cooking time, until the chicken is cooked through and golden brown on the outside.
5. Serve: Once cooked, remove the honey garlic chicken from the air fryer and let it cool slightly. Garnish with sesame seeds and chopped green onions if desired.
6. Enjoy: Serve the air fryer honey garlic chicken hot with steamed rice, quinoa, or your favorite side dish. Enjoy!

This air-fried honey garlic chicken is sweet, savory, and packed with flavor. It's sure to become a family favorite! Feel free to customize the recipe by adding your favorite vegetables or adjusting the seasoning to suit your taste.

Air Fryer Stuffed Peppers

Ingredients:

- 4 large bell peppers, any color
- 1 lb ground meat (beef, turkey, chicken, or plant-based alternative)
- 1 cup cooked rice (white, brown, or cauliflower rice for a low-carb option)
- 1 small onion, diced
- 2 cloves garlic, minced
- 1 cup diced tomatoes (fresh or canned)
- 1 cup shredded cheese (such as cheddar or mozzarella)
- 1 teaspoon dried Italian herbs (basil, oregano, thyme)
- Salt and pepper, to taste
- Cooking spray

Instructions:

1. Prepare the Bell Peppers: Cut the tops off the bell peppers and remove the seeds and membranes from the inside. Rinse the peppers under cold water and pat them dry with paper towels.
2. Cook the Filling: In a skillet, cook the ground meat over medium heat until browned and cooked through. Drain any excess fat from the skillet. Add the diced onion and minced garlic to the skillet and cook for another 2-3 minutes until softened.
3. Mix the Filling: Stir in the cooked rice, diced tomatoes, shredded cheese, dried Italian herbs, salt, and pepper into the skillet with the cooked meat mixture. Mix until well combined.
4. Stuff the Peppers: Spoon the filling mixture into the hollowed-out bell peppers, packing it down firmly. Make sure to distribute the filling evenly among the peppers.
5. Preheat the Air Fryer: Preheat your air fryer to 370°F (187°C) for 5 minutes.
6. Air Fry: Lightly coat the air fryer basket with cooking spray. Place the stuffed peppers in the air fryer basket, standing them upright. Cook in the air fryer at 370°F (187°C) for 20-25 minutes or until the peppers are tender and the filling is heated through.
7. Serve: Once cooked, remove the stuffed peppers from the air fryer and let them cool slightly before serving. Garnish with fresh herbs or additional shredded cheese if desired.

8. Enjoy: Serve the air fryer stuffed peppers hot as a delicious and nutritious meal. Enjoy!

These air-fried stuffed peppers are hearty, flavorful, and make a satisfying meal for lunch or dinner. Feel free to customize the filling with your favorite ingredients such as beans, quinoa, or different vegetables.

Air Fryer Coconut-Crusted Chicken Tenders

Ingredients:

- 1 lb chicken breast tenders or strips
- 1/2 cup shredded coconut (unsweetened)
- 1/2 cup panko breadcrumbs
- 1/4 cup all-purpose flour
- 1 teaspoon garlic powder
- 1 teaspoon onion powder
- 1/2 teaspoon paprika
- 1/2 teaspoon salt
- 1/4 teaspoon black pepper
- 2 eggs, beaten
- Cooking spray

Instructions:

1. Preheat the Air Fryer: Preheat your air fryer to 380°F (190°C) for 5 minutes.
2. Prepare the Breading Station: In three separate shallow bowls, place the all-purpose flour in the first bowl, beaten eggs in the second bowl, and a mixture of shredded coconut, panko breadcrumbs, garlic powder, onion powder, paprika, salt, and black pepper in the third bowl.
3. Coat the Chicken: Pat the chicken tenders dry with paper towels. Dredge each chicken tender in the flour, shaking off any excess. Dip it into the beaten eggs, allowing any excess to drip off. Finally, coat it with the coconut-panko mixture, pressing gently to adhere. Repeat with the remaining chicken tenders.
4. Air Fry: Lightly coat the air fryer basket with cooking spray. Arrange the coated chicken tenders in a single layer in the air fryer basket, making sure they are not touching each other. You may need to cook them in batches depending on the size of your air fryer.
5. Air Fry the Chicken: Air fry the coconut-crusted chicken tenders at 380°F (190°C) for 10-12 minutes, flipping halfway through the cooking time, until they are golden brown and cooked through.
6. Serve: Once cooked, remove the chicken tenders from the air fryer and let them cool slightly before serving. Serve them with your favorite dipping sauce, such as sweet chili sauce, barbecue sauce, or honey mustard.
7. Enjoy: Enjoy these crispy and flavorful air fryer coconut-crusted chicken tenders as a delicious appetizer or main dish!

These air-fried chicken tenders are crispy on the outside, tender and juicy on the inside, and packed with coconut flavor. They're sure to be a hit with family and friends!

Air Fryer Balsamic Brussels Sprouts

Ingredients:

- 1 lb Brussels sprouts, trimmed and halved
- 2 tablespoons olive oil
- 2 tablespoons balsamic vinegar
- 2 cloves garlic, minced
- 1 teaspoon honey or maple syrup (optional)
- Salt and pepper, to taste

Instructions:

1. Prepare the Brussels Sprouts: Trim the ends of the Brussels sprouts and cut them in half lengthwise.
2. Marinate the Brussels Sprouts: In a large bowl, whisk together the olive oil, balsamic vinegar, minced garlic, honey or maple syrup (if using), salt, and pepper. Add the halved Brussels sprouts to the bowl and toss until they are evenly coated with the marinade.
3. Preheat the Air Fryer: Preheat your air fryer to 375°F (190°C) for 5 minutes.
4. Air Fry the Brussels Sprouts: Lightly coat the air fryer basket with cooking spray. Place the marinated Brussels sprouts in the air fryer basket in a single layer, making sure they are not overcrowded. You may need to cook them in batches depending on the size of your air fryer.
5. Air Fry: Air fry the Brussels sprouts at 375°F (190°C) for 12-15 minutes, shaking the basket halfway through the cooking time, until they are tender and caramelized on the outside.
6. Serve: Once cooked, remove the Brussels sprouts from the air fryer and transfer them to a serving dish. Drizzle any remaining marinade from the bowl over the Brussels sprouts for extra flavor.
7. Enjoy: Serve the air fryer balsamic Brussels sprouts hot as a delicious and nutritious side dish for any meal!

These air-fried Brussels sprouts are crispy on the outside, tender on the inside, and bursting with sweet and tangy balsamic flavor. They're sure to be a hit with family and friends!

Air Fryer Tofu Nuggets

Ingredients:

- 1 block (14-16 oz) extra-firm tofu, pressed and drained
- 1/4 cup all-purpose flour (or cornstarch for a gluten-free option)
- 1/4 cup breadcrumbs (panko or regular)
- 1 tablespoon nutritional yeast (optional, for added flavor)
- 1 teaspoon garlic powder
- 1 teaspoon onion powder
- 1/2 teaspoon smoked paprika
- 1/2 teaspoon salt
- 1/4 teaspoon black pepper
- 2 tablespoons soy sauce or tamari
- 2 tablespoons olive oil
- Cooking spray

Instructions:

1. Prepare the Tofu: Press the tofu to remove excess moisture. Cut the pressed tofu into bite-sized nuggets or strips.
2. Prepare the Breading Mixture: In a shallow bowl, combine the all-purpose flour, breadcrumbs, nutritional yeast (if using), garlic powder, onion powder, smoked paprika, salt, and black pepper. Mix well to combine.
3. Coat the Tofu: In another shallow bowl, whisk together the soy sauce and olive oil. Dip each tofu nugget into the soy sauce mixture, then dredge it in the breadcrumb mixture, pressing gently to adhere. Repeat with the remaining tofu nuggets.
4. Preheat the Air Fryer: Preheat your air fryer to 375°F (190°C) for 5 minutes.
5. Air Fry the Tofu Nuggets: Lightly coat the air fryer basket with cooking spray. Place the breaded tofu nuggets in the air fryer basket in a single layer, making sure they are not touching each other. You may need to cook them in batches depending on the size of your air fryer.
6. Air Fry: Air fry the tofu nuggets at 375°F (190°C) for 10-12 minutes, flipping halfway through the cooking time, until they are golden brown and crispy on the outside.
7. Serve: Once cooked, remove the tofu nuggets from the air fryer and let them cool slightly before serving. Serve them with your favorite dipping sauce, such as barbecue sauce, ketchup, or honey mustard.

8. Enjoy: Enjoy these crispy and flavorful air fryer tofu nuggets as a delicious and nutritious snack or meal!

These air-fried tofu nuggets are crispy on the outside, tender on the inside, and packed with savory flavor from the seasoned breadcrumb coating. They're sure to be a hit with vegetarians and meat-eaters alike!

Air Fryer Roasted Garlic Potatoes

Ingredients:

- 1.5 lbs baby potatoes, halved or quartered
- 2 tablespoons olive oil
- 4 cloves garlic, minced
- 1 teaspoon dried thyme
- 1 teaspoon dried rosemary
- Salt and pepper, to taste
- Chopped fresh parsley, for garnish (optional)

Instructions:

1. Preheat the Air Fryer: Preheat your air fryer to 400°F (200°C) for 5 minutes.
2. Prepare the Potatoes: In a large bowl, toss the halved or quartered baby potatoes with olive oil, minced garlic, dried thyme, dried rosemary, salt, and pepper until the potatoes are evenly coated with the seasoning mixture.
3. Air Fry the Potatoes: Lightly coat the air fryer basket with cooking spray. Place the seasoned potatoes in the air fryer basket in a single layer, making sure they are not overcrowded. You may need to cook them in batches depending on the size of your air fryer.
4. Air Fry: Air fry the potatoes at 400°F (200°C) for 20-25 minutes, shaking the basket halfway through the cooking time, until the potatoes are golden brown and crispy on the outside and tender on the inside.
5. Serve: Once cooked, remove the roasted garlic potatoes from the air fryer and transfer them to a serving dish. Garnish with chopped fresh parsley if desired.
6. Enjoy: Serve the air fryer roasted garlic potatoes hot as a delicious side dish for any meal!

These air-fried garlic potatoes are crispy, flavorful, and packed with savory garlic and herb flavor. They're sure to be a hit with family and friends! Feel free to customize the seasoning with your favorite herbs and spices for added variety.

Air Fryer Chicken Satay Skewers

Ingredients:

- 1 lb boneless, skinless chicken breasts or thighs, cut into thin strips
- 1/4 cup coconut milk
- 2 tablespoons soy sauce
- 2 tablespoons brown sugar
- 1 tablespoon lime juice
- 2 cloves garlic, minced
- 1 teaspoon ground coriander
- 1/2 teaspoon ground turmeric
- 1/2 teaspoon ground cumin
- 1/4 teaspoon cayenne pepper (optional, for heat)
- Salt and pepper, to taste
- Wooden skewers, soaked in water for at least 30 minutes

Instructions:

1. Marinate the Chicken: In a bowl, combine the coconut milk, soy sauce, brown sugar, lime juice, minced garlic, ground coriander, ground turmeric, ground cumin, cayenne pepper (if using), salt, and pepper. Add the chicken strips to the marinade and toss until they are evenly coated. Cover the bowl and let the chicken marinate in the refrigerator for at least 30 minutes, or overnight for best results.
2. Preheat the Air Fryer: Preheat your air fryer to 400°F (200°C) for 5 minutes.
3. Thread the Chicken: Thread the marinated chicken strips onto the soaked wooden skewers, leaving a little space between each piece.
4. Air Fry: Lightly coat the air fryer basket with cooking spray. Place the chicken skewers in the air fryer basket in a single layer, making sure they are not touching each other. You may need to cook them in batches depending on the size of your air fryer.
5. Air Fry the Chicken Satay: Air fry the chicken skewers at 400°F (200°C) for 10-12 minutes, flipping halfway through the cooking time, until the chicken is cooked through and lightly charred on the edges.
6. Serve: Once cooked, remove the chicken satay skewers from the air fryer and let them cool slightly before serving. Serve them with your favorite dipping sauce, such as peanut sauce, sweet chili sauce, or cucumber salad.

7. Enjoy: Enjoy these delicious air fryer chicken satay skewers as a flavorful appetizer or main dish that's perfect for any occasion!

These air-fried chicken satay skewers are tender, juicy, and packed with aromatic spices and flavors. They're sure to be a hit with family and friends! Feel free to customize the marinade with your favorite herbs and spices for added variety.

Air Fryer Kale Chips

Ingredients:

- 1 bunch kale, washed and thoroughly dried
- 1 tablespoon olive oil
- Salt, to taste
- Optional seasonings: garlic powder, onion powder, paprika, nutritional yeast, etc.

Instructions:

1. Prepare the Kale: Remove the tough stems from the kale leaves and tear the leaves into bite-sized pieces. Make sure the kale leaves are completely dry before proceeding.
2. Massage with Olive Oil: In a large bowl, drizzle the kale pieces with olive oil. Use your hands to massage the oil into the kale leaves, making sure they are evenly coated.
3. Season the Kale: Sprinkle the kale with salt and any optional seasonings of your choice, such as garlic powder, onion powder, paprika, or nutritional yeast. Toss the kale gently to distribute the seasonings evenly.
4. Preheat the Air Fryer: Preheat your air fryer to 350°F (175°C) for 5 minutes.
5. Air Fry: Lightly coat the air fryer basket with cooking spray. Arrange the seasoned kale leaves in a single layer in the air fryer basket, making sure they are not overlapping.
6. Air Fry the Kale: Air fry the kale at 350°F (175°C) for 5-7 minutes, shaking the basket halfway through the cooking time, until the kale is crispy and lightly browned. Keep a close eye on the kale during the last few minutes of cooking to prevent burning.
7. Serve: Once cooked, remove the kale chips from the air fryer and let them cool slightly before serving. Enjoy them immediately as a crispy and nutritious snack!

These air-fried kale chips are crunchy, flavorful, and packed with vitamins and minerals. They're a great alternative to potato chips and perfect for snacking on-the-go or as a guilt-free movie night treat. Feel free to experiment with different seasonings to customize the flavor to your liking!

Air Fryer Orange Chicken

Ingredients:

- 1 lb boneless, skinless chicken breasts, cut into bite-sized pieces
- 1/2 cup orange juice
- Zest of 1 orange
- 3 tablespoons soy sauce
- 2 tablespoons honey
- 1 tablespoon rice vinegar
- 1 tablespoon cornstarch
- 1 teaspoon sesame oil
- 2 cloves garlic, minced
- 1/2 teaspoon ground ginger
- 1/4 teaspoon red pepper flakes (optional, for heat)
- Salt and pepper, to taste
- Sesame seeds and sliced green onions, for garnish (optional)

Instructions:

1. Prepare the Sauce: In a small bowl, whisk together the orange juice, orange zest, soy sauce, honey, rice vinegar, cornstarch, sesame oil, minced garlic, ground ginger, red pepper flakes (if using), salt, and pepper until well combined. Set aside.
2. Marinate the Chicken: Place the bite-sized chicken pieces in a bowl or resealable plastic bag. Pour half of the prepared sauce over the chicken and toss to coat. Let the chicken marinate in the refrigerator for at least 30 minutes, or overnight for best results.
3. Preheat the Air Fryer: Preheat your air fryer to 380°F (190°C) for 5 minutes.
4. Air Fry the Chicken: Lightly coat the air fryer basket with cooking spray. Place the marinated chicken pieces in the air fryer basket in a single layer, making sure they are not overcrowded. You may need to cook them in batches depending on the size of your air fryer.
5. Air Fry: Air fry the chicken at 380°F (190°C) for 10-12 minutes, flipping halfway through the cooking time, until the chicken is cooked through and golden brown on the outside.
6. Warm the Sauce: While the chicken is cooking, transfer the remaining sauce to a small saucepan. Bring the sauce to a simmer over medium heat, stirring frequently, until it thickens slightly.

7. Coat the Chicken: Once the chicken is cooked, transfer it to a large bowl. Pour the warmed sauce over the cooked chicken and toss to coat evenly.
8. Serve: Once coated, transfer the air fryer orange chicken to a serving dish. Garnish with sesame seeds and sliced green onions if desired.
9. Enjoy: Serve the air fryer orange chicken hot with steamed rice or noodles. Enjoy!

This air-fried orange chicken is crispy, tangy, and bursting with citrus flavor. It's sure to be a hit with family and friends! Feel free to customize the recipe by adding your favorite vegetables such as bell peppers, broccoli, or snap peas.

Air Fryer Ratatouille

Ingredients:

- 1 medium eggplant, diced
- 1 medium zucchini, diced
- 1 medium yellow squash, diced
- 1 red bell pepper, diced
- 1 yellow bell pepper, diced
- 1 onion, diced
- 2 cloves garlic, minced
- 2 tablespoons olive oil
- 1 can (14 oz) diced tomatoes
- 1 teaspoon dried thyme
- 1 teaspoon dried oregano
- Salt and pepper, to taste
- Fresh basil, chopped, for garnish

Instructions:

1. Prepare the Vegetables: Place the diced eggplant, zucchini, yellow squash, red bell pepper, yellow bell pepper, onion, and minced garlic in a large bowl. Drizzle with olive oil and toss until the vegetables are evenly coated.
2. Season the Vegetables: Season the vegetables with dried thyme, dried oregano, salt, and pepper. Toss again to coat the vegetables with the seasoning.
3. Preheat the Air Fryer: Preheat your air fryer to 375°F (190°C) for 5 minutes.
4. Air Fry the Vegetables: Lightly coat the air fryer basket with cooking spray. Place the seasoned vegetables in the air fryer basket in a single layer, making sure they are not overcrowded. You may need to cook them in batches depending on the size of your air fryer.
5. Air Fry: Air fry the vegetables at 375°F (190°C) for 12-15 minutes, shaking the basket halfway through the cooking time, until the vegetables are tender and lightly browned.
6. Add the Tomatoes: Once the vegetables are cooked, add the diced tomatoes to the air fryer basket. Toss gently to combine with the cooked vegetables.
7. Cook Together: Continue to air fry the vegetables and tomatoes together for an additional 3-5 minutes, until the tomatoes are heated through.
8. Serve: Once cooked, remove the ratatouille from the air fryer and transfer it to a serving dish. Garnish with chopped fresh basil before serving.

9. Enjoy: Serve the air fryer ratatouille hot as a delicious and nutritious side dish or vegetarian main course. Enjoy!

This air-fried ratatouille is flavorful, colorful, and packed with vitamins and minerals from the fresh vegetables. It's a great way to enjoy a taste of summer any time of year! Feel free to customize the recipe by adding other vegetables such as mushrooms, cherry tomatoes, or artichoke hearts.

Air Fryer Chicken Fajitas

Ingredients:

- 1 lb boneless, skinless chicken breasts, thinly sliced
- 2 bell peppers (any color), sliced
- 1 onion, sliced
- 2 tablespoons olive oil
- 2 tablespoons fajita seasoning (store-bought or homemade)
- Salt and pepper, to taste
- Flour or corn tortillas, for serving
- Optional toppings: shredded cheese, salsa, guacamole, sour cream, chopped cilantro, lime wedges, etc.

Instructions:

1. Preheat the Air Fryer: Preheat your air fryer to 400°F (200°C) for 5 minutes.
2. Prepare the Chicken and Vegetables: In a large bowl, combine the sliced chicken breasts, sliced bell peppers, and sliced onion. Drizzle with olive oil and sprinkle with fajita seasoning, salt, and pepper. Toss until the chicken and vegetables are evenly coated with the seasoning mixture.
3. Air Fry: Lightly coat the air fryer basket with cooking spray. Place the seasoned chicken and vegetables in the air fryer basket in a single layer, making sure they are not overcrowded. You may need to cook them in batches depending on the size of your air fryer.
4. Air Fry the Chicken Fajitas: Air fry the chicken and vegetables at 400°F (200°C) for 12-15 minutes, shaking the basket halfway through the cooking time, until the chicken is cooked through and the vegetables are tender and slightly charred.
5. Warm the Tortillas: While the chicken and vegetables are cooking, warm the tortillas in the microwave or on a skillet until they are soft and pliable.
6. Serve: Once cooked, remove the chicken and vegetables from the air fryer and transfer them to a serving dish. Serve the chicken fajitas with warm tortillas and your favorite toppings.
7. Enjoy: Let everyone assemble their own fajitas at the table, adding their desired toppings. Enjoy these delicious air fryer chicken fajitas as a quick and satisfying meal!

These air-fried chicken fajitas are flavorful, tender, and packed with vibrant colors and textures. They're sure to be a hit with family and friends! Feel free to customize the recipe by adding other toppings such as sliced jalapenos, diced tomatoes, or black beans.

Air Fryer Butternut Squash Fries

Ingredients:

- 1 medium butternut squash
- 2 tablespoons olive oil
- 1 teaspoon garlic powder
- 1 teaspoon paprika
- 1/2 teaspoon cumin
- Salt and pepper, to taste
- Optional: grated Parmesan cheese, chopped fresh herbs (such as parsley or rosemary)

Instructions:

1. Preheat the Air Fryer: Preheat your air fryer to 400°F (200°C) for 5 minutes.
2. Prepare the Butternut Squash: Peel the butternut squash and cut off the ends. Cut the squash in half crosswise where the neck meets the bulbous base. Slice the neck portion into fries about 1/2 inch thick. You can also cut the base portion into fries, discarding the seeds.
3. Season the Fries: In a large bowl, toss the butternut squash fries with olive oil, garlic powder, paprika, cumin, salt, and pepper until evenly coated.
4. Arrange in the Air Fryer: Lightly coat the air fryer basket with cooking spray. Arrange the seasoned butternut squash fries in a single layer in the air fryer basket, making sure they are not overcrowded. You may need to cook them in batches depending on the size of your air fryer.
5. Air Fry: Air fry the butternut squash fries at 400°F (200°C) for 15-20 minutes, shaking the basket halfway through the cooking time, until the fries are golden brown and crispy on the outside and tender on the inside.
6. Optional Toppings: If desired, sprinkle the cooked butternut squash fries with grated Parmesan cheese and chopped fresh herbs before serving.
7. Serve: Once cooked, remove the butternut squash fries from the air fryer and transfer them to a serving dish. Serve them hot as a delicious and nutritious side dish or snack!

These air-fried butternut squash fries are crispy, flavorful, and packed with vitamins and minerals. They're sure to be a hit with family and friends! Feel free to customize the seasoning to your liking or serve them with your favorite dipping sauce.

Air Fryer Korean BBQ Wings

Ingredients:

- 2 lbs chicken wings, split into drumettes and flats
- 1/4 cup soy sauce
- 2 tablespoons brown sugar
- 2 tablespoons rice vinegar
- 2 tablespoons sesame oil
- 2 cloves garlic, minced
- 1 teaspoon grated ginger
- 1 tablespoon gochujang (Korean chili paste) or sriracha (optional, for heat)
- Sesame seeds and chopped green onions, for garnish
- Cooking spray

Instructions:

1. Marinate the Wings: In a large bowl, whisk together the soy sauce, brown sugar, rice vinegar, sesame oil, minced garlic, grated ginger, and gochujang or sriracha (if using). Add the chicken wings to the bowl and toss until they are evenly coated with the marinade. Cover the bowl and let the wings marinate in the refrigerator for at least 1 hour, or overnight for best results.
2. Preheat the Air Fryer: Preheat your air fryer to 380°F (190°C) for 5 minutes.
3. Air Fry the Wings: Lightly coat the air fryer basket with cooking spray. Place the marinated chicken wings in the air fryer basket in a single layer, making sure they are not overcrowded. You may need to cook them in batches depending on the size of your air fryer.
4. Air Fry: Air fry the wings at 380°F (190°C) for 25-30 minutes, flipping halfway through the cooking time, until they are golden brown and crispy on the outside and cooked through on the inside.
5. Garnish and Serve: Once cooked, remove the wings from the air fryer and transfer them to a serving dish. Garnish with sesame seeds and chopped green onions.
6. Enjoy: Serve the air fryer Korean BBQ wings hot as a delicious appetizer or main dish. Enjoy!

These air-fried Korean BBQ wings are sweet, savory, and packed with flavor. They're sure to be a hit at your next party or game day gathering! Feel free to adjust the amount of gochujang or sriracha to suit your taste preferences.

Air Fryer Quinoa-Stuffed Bell Peppers

Ingredients:

- 4 large bell peppers (any color), tops removed and seeds removed
- 1 cup quinoa, rinsed
- 2 cups vegetable broth or water
- 1 tablespoon olive oil
- 1 onion, diced
- 2 cloves garlic, minced
- 1 carrot, diced
- 1 zucchini, diced
- 1 cup diced tomatoes (fresh or canned)
- 1 teaspoon dried oregano
- 1 teaspoon dried basil
- Salt and pepper, to taste
- 1 cup shredded cheese (such as mozzarella or cheddar)
- Chopped fresh parsley or basil, for garnish (optional)

Instructions:

1. Cook the Quinoa: In a medium saucepan, combine the quinoa and vegetable broth or water. Bring to a boil, then reduce the heat to low, cover, and simmer for 15-20 minutes, or until the quinoa is cooked and the liquid is absorbed.
2. Prepare the Bell Peppers: While the quinoa is cooking, prepare the bell peppers. Cut off the tops of the bell peppers and remove the seeds and membranes from the inside. Rinse the peppers under cold water and pat them dry with paper towels.
3. Prepare the Filling: In a large skillet, heat the olive oil over medium heat. Add the diced onion and cook for 2-3 minutes until softened. Add the minced garlic, diced carrot, and diced zucchini to the skillet and cook for another 5 minutes, until the vegetables are tender. Stir in the diced tomatoes, dried oregano, dried basil, salt, and pepper. Cook for an additional 2-3 minutes, then remove the skillet from the heat.
4. Combine the Filling: In a large bowl, combine the cooked quinoa and the cooked vegetable mixture. Stir until well combined.
5. Stuff the Bell Peppers: Divide the quinoa and vegetable mixture evenly among the hollowed-out bell peppers, packing it down firmly. Place the stuffed bell peppers in the air fryer basket.

6. Air Fry: Preheat your air fryer to 370°F (187°C) for 5 minutes. Once preheated, place the stuffed bell peppers in the air fryer basket and cook at 370°F (187°C) for 20-25 minutes, or until the bell peppers are tender.
7. Add Cheese and Garnish: In the last 5 minutes of cooking, sprinkle the shredded cheese over the tops of the stuffed bell peppers. Allow the cheese to melt and become bubbly.
8. Serve: Once cooked, remove the stuffed bell peppers from the air fryer and let them cool slightly before serving. Garnish with chopped fresh parsley or basil, if desired.
9. Enjoy: Serve the air fryer quinoa-stuffed bell peppers hot as a nutritious and satisfying meal. Enjoy!

These air-fried quinoa-stuffed bell peppers are flavorful, filling, and packed with healthy ingredients. They're perfect for a meatless dinner option or for anyone looking to incorporate more plant-based meals into their diet. Feel free to customize the filling with your favorite vegetables and herbs.

Air Fryer Veggie Spring Rolls

Ingredients:

- 10 spring roll wrappers
- 2 cups shredded cabbage
- 1 cup shredded carrots
- 1 cup shredded bell peppers (any color)
- 1 cup bean sprouts
- 2 green onions, thinly sliced
- 2 tablespoons soy sauce or tamari
- 1 tablespoon sesame oil
- 1 teaspoon grated ginger
- 1 clove garlic, minced
- 1 tablespoon cornstarch mixed with 2 tablespoons water (for sealing the spring rolls)
- Cooking spray

Instructions:

1. Prepare the Filling: In a large bowl, combine the shredded cabbage, shredded carrots, shredded bell peppers, bean sprouts, and sliced green onions. In a small bowl, whisk together the soy sauce, sesame oil, grated ginger, and minced garlic. Pour the sauce over the vegetable mixture and toss until well combined.
2. Assemble the Spring Rolls: Place a spring roll wrapper on a clean, flat surface, with one corner facing towards you (like a diamond shape). Spoon about 2-3 tablespoons of the vegetable filling onto the bottom third of the wrapper, leaving a border on either side. Fold the bottom corner over the filling, then fold in the sides, and roll up tightly. Brush the top corner of the wrapper with the cornstarch mixture to seal the spring roll. Repeat with the remaining wrappers and filling.
3. Preheat the Air Fryer: Preheat your air fryer to 375°F (190°C) for 5 minutes.
4. Air Fry the Spring Rolls: Lightly coat the air fryer basket with cooking spray. Place the assembled spring rolls in the air fryer basket in a single layer, making sure they are not touching each other. You may need to cook them in batches depending on the size of your air fryer. Spray the tops of the spring rolls with cooking spray.
5. Air Fry: Air fry the spring rolls at 375°F (190°C) for 10-12 minutes, flipping halfway through the cooking time, until they are golden brown and crispy.

6. Serve: Once cooked, remove the spring rolls from the air fryer and let them cool slightly before serving. Serve them with your favorite dipping sauce, such as sweet chili sauce, soy sauce, or hoisin sauce.
7. Enjoy: Enjoy these crispy and flavorful air fryer veggie spring rolls as a delicious appetizer or snack!

These air-fried veggie spring rolls are a healthier alternative to traditional deep-fried spring rolls, and they're packed with fresh and colorful vegetables. They're perfect for parties, potlucks, or as a light meal. Feel free to customize the filling with your favorite veggies or add cooked protein like tofu or shrimp for extra flavor and protein.

Air Fryer Parmesan Crusted Asparagus

Ingredients:

- 1 bunch asparagus, woody ends trimmed
- 1/4 cup grated Parmesan cheese
- 1/4 cup panko breadcrumbs
- 1 tablespoon olive oil
- 1/2 teaspoon garlic powder
- Salt and pepper, to taste
- Cooking spray

Instructions:

1. Preheat the Air Fryer: Preheat your air fryer to 400°F (200°C) for 5 minutes.
2. Prepare the Asparagus: In a shallow dish, combine the grated Parmesan cheese, panko breadcrumbs, olive oil, garlic powder, salt, and pepper. Mix well to combine.
3. Coat the Asparagus: Lightly coat the asparagus spears with cooking spray. Dip each asparagus spear into the Parmesan mixture, coating it evenly on all sides. Press gently to adhere the mixture to the asparagus.
4. Arrange in the Air Fryer: Place the coated asparagus spears in the air fryer basket in a single layer, making sure they are not overlapping.
5. Air Fry: Air fry the asparagus at 400°F (200°C) for 8-10 minutes, or until the coating is golden brown and crispy, and the asparagus is tender-crisp. You may need to shake the basket halfway through the cooking time for even cooking.
6. Serve: Once cooked, remove the Parmesan crusted asparagus from the air fryer and transfer them to a serving dish.
7. Enjoy: Serve the air fryer Parmesan crusted asparagus hot as a delicious and flavorful side dish!

This air-fried Parmesan crusted asparagus is crispy, flavorful, and packed with cheesy goodness. It's a perfect way to enjoy fresh asparagus in a new and exciting way. Feel free to customize the seasoning or add additional toppings like lemon zest or chopped herbs for extra flavor.

Air Fryer Jamaican Jerk Chicken

Ingredients:

- 4 bone-in, skin-on chicken thighs
- 2 tablespoons Jamaican jerk seasoning
- 1 tablespoon olive oil
- 1 tablespoon soy sauce or tamari
- 1 tablespoon lime juice
- 1 teaspoon honey or maple syrup
- Salt and pepper, to taste
- Cooking spray

Instructions:

1. Marinate the Chicken: In a large bowl, combine the Jamaican jerk seasoning, olive oil, soy sauce or tamari, lime juice, honey or maple syrup, salt, and pepper. Mix well to form a marinade. Add the chicken thighs to the bowl and toss until they are evenly coated with the marinade. Cover the bowl and let the chicken marinate in the refrigerator for at least 1 hour, or overnight for best results.
2. Preheat the Air Fryer: Preheat your air fryer to 375°F (190°C) for 5 minutes.
3. Arrange the Chicken in the Air Fryer: Lightly coat the air fryer basket with cooking spray. Place the marinated chicken thighs in the air fryer basket, skin side down.
4. Air Fry the Chicken: Air fry the chicken thighs at 375°F (190°C) for 12-15 minutes, flipping halfway through the cooking time, until the chicken is cooked through and the skin is crispy and golden brown.
5. Check for Doneness: Use a meat thermometer to ensure that the internal temperature of the chicken reaches 165°F (75°C) at the thickest part.
6. Serve: Once cooked, remove the Jamaican jerk chicken thighs from the air fryer and let them rest for a few minutes before serving.
7. Enjoy: Serve the air fryer Jamaican jerk chicken hot with your favorite sides, such as rice and peas, grilled vegetables, or coleslaw. Enjoy!

This air-fried Jamaican jerk chicken is tender, juicy, and packed with bold flavors. It's a delicious and convenient way to enjoy this classic Caribbean dish without the need for a grill. Feel free to adjust the amount of Jamaican jerk seasoning to suit your taste preferences, and serve with additional lime wedges for a burst of freshness.

Air Fryer Stuffed Mushrooms

Ingredients:

- 12 large mushrooms, stems removed and reserved
- 1/2 cup cream cheese, softened
- 1/4 cup grated Parmesan cheese
- 2 cloves garlic, minced
- 2 tablespoons chopped fresh parsley
- 1/4 teaspoon dried oregano
- Salt and pepper, to taste
- Olive oil or cooking spray

Instructions:

1. Prepare the Mushrooms: Clean the mushrooms by wiping them with a damp paper towel. Gently remove the stems from the mushrooms and chop them finely. Set the mushroom caps aside.
2. Prepare the Filling: In a mixing bowl, combine the softened cream cheese, grated Parmesan cheese, minced garlic, chopped parsley, dried oregano, chopped mushroom stems, salt, and pepper. Mix until well combined.
3. Stuff the Mushrooms: Using a small spoon or your fingers, fill each mushroom cap with the cream cheese mixture, pressing it down gently to compact the filling and create a mound on top.
4. Preheat the Air Fryer: Preheat your air fryer to 360°F (180°C) for 5 minutes.
5. Arrange in the Air Fryer: Lightly grease the air fryer basket with olive oil or cooking spray. Place the stuffed mushrooms in the air fryer basket in a single layer, making sure they are not touching each other.
6. Air Fry: Air fry the stuffed mushrooms at 360°F (180°C) for 8-10 minutes, or until the mushrooms are tender and the filling is golden brown and bubbly.
7. Serve: Once cooked, remove the stuffed mushrooms from the air fryer and let them cool slightly before serving.
8. Enjoy: Serve the air fryer stuffed mushrooms hot as a delicious appetizer or side dish. Garnish with additional chopped parsley or grated Parmesan cheese, if desired. Enjoy!

These air-fried stuffed mushrooms are savory, creamy, and incredibly flavorful. They're perfect for entertaining guests or as a tasty snack for yourself. Feel free to customize the filling with your favorite ingredients, such as cooked bacon, chopped spinach, or sun-dried tomatoes.

Air Fryer Lemon Herb Tofu

Ingredients:

- 1 block (14-16 oz) extra-firm tofu, pressed and drained
- 2 tablespoons olive oil
- 2 tablespoons fresh lemon juice
- Zest of 1 lemon
- 2 cloves garlic, minced
- 1 tablespoon chopped fresh herbs (such as parsley, thyme, or rosemary)
- Salt and pepper, to taste

Instructions:

1. Prepare the Tofu: Slice the pressed and drained tofu into cubes or strips, depending on your preference.
2. Marinate the Tofu: In a mixing bowl, combine the olive oil, fresh lemon juice, lemon zest, minced garlic, chopped fresh herbs, salt, and pepper. Whisk until well combined. Add the tofu cubes or strips to the bowl and gently toss until they are evenly coated with the marinade. Let the tofu marinate for at least 15-30 minutes to allow the flavors to meld.
3. Preheat the Air Fryer: Preheat your air fryer to 375°F (190°C) for 5 minutes.
4. Arrange in the Air Fryer: Lightly grease the air fryer basket with cooking spray or a small amount of olive oil. Arrange the marinated tofu cubes or strips in a single layer in the air fryer basket, making sure they are not overcrowded. You may need to cook them in batches depending on the size of your air fryer.
5. Air Fry the Tofu: Air fry the tofu at 375°F (190°C) for 15-20 minutes, shaking the basket halfway through the cooking time, until the tofu is golden brown and crispy on the outside, and tender on the inside.
6. Serve: Once cooked, remove the lemon herb tofu from the air fryer and transfer it to a serving dish.
7. Enjoy: Serve the air fryer lemon herb tofu hot as a delicious and protein-rich main dish or add it to salads, stir-fries, or grain bowls. Enjoy!

This air-fried lemon herb tofu is tangy, aromatic, and packed with fresh flavors. It's a versatile dish that can be enjoyed on its own or incorporated into a variety of recipes.

Feel free to adjust the seasonings to suit your taste preferences, and experiment with different herbs and spices for a unique twist.

Air Fryer Green Bean Fries

Ingredients:

- 1 lb fresh green beans, ends trimmed
- 1/2 cup all-purpose flour (or almond flour for a gluten-free option)
- 2 eggs, beaten
- 1 cup breadcrumbs (or panko breadcrumbs for extra crunch)
- 1/4 cup grated Parmesan cheese (optional)
- 1 teaspoon garlic powder
- 1 teaspoon paprika
- Salt and pepper, to taste
- Cooking spray

Instructions:

1. Prepare the Green Beans: Rinse the green beans under cold water and pat them dry with paper towels. Trim off the ends if needed.
2. Set Up Breading Station: In three separate shallow dishes, place the flour in one, beaten eggs in another, and breadcrumbs mixed with grated Parmesan cheese (if using), garlic powder, paprika, salt, and pepper in the third.
3. Coat the Green Beans: Working in batches, dredge the green beans in the flour, shaking off any excess. Dip them into the beaten eggs, allowing any excess to drip off. Then, coat them evenly with the breadcrumb mixture, pressing gently to adhere.
4. Preheat the Air Fryer: Preheat your air fryer to 380°F (190°C) for 5 minutes.
5. Arrange in the Air Fryer: Lightly grease the air fryer basket with cooking spray. Place the breaded green beans in the basket in a single layer, making sure they are not touching or overlapping.
6. Air Fry: Air fry the green bean fries at 380°F (190°C) for 8-10 minutes, shaking the basket halfway through the cooking time, until they are golden brown and crispy.
7. Serve: Once cooked, remove the green bean fries from the air fryer and transfer them to a serving dish.
8. Enjoy: Serve the air fryer green bean fries hot as a delicious and nutritious appetizer or side dish. Enjoy!

These air-fried green bean fries are crispy on the outside and tender on the inside, making them a perfect snack or accompaniment to any meal. Feel free to customize the seasoning to your liking or serve them with your favorite dipping sauce, such as ranch dressing or marinara sauce.

Air Fryer Cajun Shrimp

Ingredients:

- 1 lb large shrimp, peeled and deveined
- 2 tablespoons olive oil
- 2 tablespoons Cajun seasoning
- 1 teaspoon garlic powder
- 1 teaspoon paprika
- 1/2 teaspoon onion powder
- 1/2 teaspoon dried thyme
- 1/2 teaspoon dried oregano
- 1/4 teaspoon cayenne pepper (optional, for extra heat)
- Salt and pepper, to taste
- Lemon wedges, for serving

Instructions:

1. Preheat the Air Fryer: Preheat your air fryer to 400°F (200°C) for 5 minutes.
2. Prepare the Shrimp: In a large bowl, combine the shrimp with olive oil, Cajun seasoning, garlic powder, paprika, onion powder, dried thyme, dried oregano, cayenne pepper (if using), salt, and pepper. Toss until the shrimp are evenly coated with the seasoning mixture.
3. Arrange in the Air Fryer: Lightly grease the air fryer basket with cooking spray. Arrange the seasoned shrimp in a single layer in the air fryer basket, making sure they are not overcrowded. You may need to cook them in batches depending on the size of your air fryer.
4. Air Fry the Shrimp: Air fry the shrimp at 400°F (200°C) for 6-8 minutes, shaking the basket halfway through the cooking time, until the shrimp are pink, opaque, and cooked through.
5. Serve: Once cooked, remove the Cajun shrimp from the air fryer and transfer them to a serving platter. Squeeze fresh lemon juice over the shrimp and serve immediately.
6. Enjoy: Serve the air fryer Cajun shrimp hot as a delicious and flavorful appetizer or main dish. Enjoy!

These air-fried Cajun shrimp are spicy, smoky, and packed with bold flavors. They're perfect for serving over rice, pasta, or salad, or enjoyed on their own with your favorite dipping sauce. Feel free to adjust the amount of Cajun seasoning and cayenne pepper to suit your taste preferences.

Air Fryer Stuffed Zucchini Boats

Ingredients:

- 2 large zucchinis
- 1 tablespoon olive oil
- 1 small onion, diced
- 2 cloves garlic, minced
- 1 bell pepper, diced
- 1 cup diced tomatoes (fresh or canned)
- 1 cup cooked quinoa or rice
- 1/2 cup shredded mozzarella cheese
- 2 tablespoons grated Parmesan cheese
- 1 teaspoon Italian seasoning
- Salt and pepper, to taste
- Chopped fresh parsley or basil, for garnish (optional)

Instructions:

1. Prepare the Zucchinis: Cut the zucchinis in half lengthwise and scoop out the seeds and flesh from the center, leaving about a 1/4-inch border around the edges to create zucchini boats. Set aside.
2. Prepare the Filling: In a large skillet, heat the olive oil over medium heat. Add the diced onion and cook for 2-3 minutes until softened. Add the minced garlic and diced bell pepper to the skillet and cook for another 2-3 minutes until the bell pepper is tender. Stir in the diced tomatoes, cooked quinoa or rice, shredded mozzarella cheese, grated Parmesan cheese, Italian seasoning, salt, and pepper. Cook for an additional 2-3 minutes until everything is well combined and heated through.
3. Stuff the Zucchini Boats: Divide the filling mixture evenly among the hollowed-out zucchini boats, pressing down gently to pack the filling into the boats.
4. Preheat the Air Fryer: Preheat your air fryer to 375°F (190°C) for 5 minutes.
5. Arrange in the Air Fryer: Lightly grease the air fryer basket with cooking spray. Place the stuffed zucchini boats in the air fryer basket in a single layer, making sure they are not touching each other.
6. Air Fry: Air fry the stuffed zucchini boats at 375°F (190°C) for 12-15 minutes, or until the zucchinis are tender and the filling is heated through and golden brown on top.

7. Garnish and Serve: Once cooked, remove the stuffed zucchini boats from the air fryer and transfer them to a serving platter. Garnish with chopped fresh parsley or basil, if desired.
8. Enjoy: Serve the air fryer stuffed zucchini boats hot as a delicious and nutritious meal. Enjoy!

These air-fried stuffed zucchini boats are packed with flavor and make a satisfying vegetarian dish. Feel free to customize the filling with your favorite ingredients, such as ground meat, beans, or different types of cheese. Experiment with different herbs and spices to create your own unique flavor combinations.

Air Fryer Greek Veggie Patties

Ingredients:

- 1 can (15 oz) chickpeas, drained and rinsed
- 1 cup cooked quinoa or brown rice
- 1/2 cup finely chopped red onion
- 1/2 cup finely chopped bell pepper (any color)
- 1/4 cup chopped fresh parsley
- 2 cloves garlic, minced
- 1 teaspoon ground cumin
- 1 teaspoon dried oregano
- 1/2 teaspoon paprika
- Salt and pepper, to taste
- 1 tablespoon olive oil
- Cooking spray

Instructions:

1. Prepare the Veggie Patty Mixture: In a large mixing bowl, mash the chickpeas with a fork or potato masher until they are mostly smooth but still have some texture. Add the cooked quinoa or brown rice, finely chopped red onion, finely chopped bell pepper, chopped fresh parsley, minced garlic, ground cumin, dried oregano, paprika, salt, and pepper to the bowl. Mix until well combined.
2. Shape the Patties: Divide the veggie patty mixture into 4 equal portions. Shape each portion into a patty about 1/2-inch thick.
3. Preheat the Air Fryer: Preheat your air fryer to 375°F (190°C) for 5 minutes.
4. Arrange in the Air Fryer: Lightly grease the air fryer basket with cooking spray. Place the veggie patties in the air fryer basket in a single layer, making sure they are not touching each other.
5. Air Fry: Air fry the veggie patties at 375°F (190°C) for 12-15 minutes, flipping halfway through the cooking time, until they are golden brown and crispy on the outside.
6. Serve: Once cooked, remove the Greek veggie patties from the air fryer and let them cool slightly before serving.
7. Enjoy: Serve the air fryer Greek veggie patties hot as a delicious and nutritious main dish or as a protein-packed addition to salads, wraps, or grain bowls. Enjoy!

These air-fried Greek veggie patties are flavorful, hearty, and packed with plant-based protein. Feel free to customize the seasoning and add your favorite herbs and spices for extra flavor. You can also serve them with tzatziki sauce, hummus, or your favorite Greek-inspired condiments for dipping.

Air Fryer Cinnamon Apple Chips

Ingredients:

- 2 large apples (such as Honeycrisp or Granny Smith)
- 1 tablespoon ground cinnamon
- 1 tablespoon granulated sugar (optional)
- Cooking spray

Instructions:

1. Prepare the Apples: Wash the apples thoroughly and pat them dry with a clean towel. Use a sharp knife or a mandoline slicer to thinly slice the apples into rounds, about 1/8-inch thick. Remove and discard any seeds or stems.
2. Season the Apple Slices: In a small bowl, combine the ground cinnamon and granulated sugar (if using). Mix well to evenly distribute the cinnamon and sugar.
3. Coat the Apple Slices: Place the apple slices in a large mixing bowl. Sprinkle the cinnamon sugar mixture over the apple slices, tossing gently to coat each slice evenly.
4. Preheat the Air Fryer: Preheat your air fryer to 375°F (190°C) for 5 minutes.
5. Arrange in the Air Fryer: Lightly grease the air fryer basket with cooking spray. Arrange the seasoned apple slices in a single layer in the air fryer basket, making sure they are not overlapping or touching each other.
6. Air Fry: Air fry the apple slices at 375°F (190°C) for 8-10 minutes, flipping halfway through the cooking time, until they are golden brown and crispy.
7. Cool and Serve: Once cooked, remove the cinnamon apple chips from the air fryer and let them cool on a wire rack for a few minutes. They will continue to crisp up as they cool.
8. Enjoy: Serve the air fryer cinnamon apple chips as a delicious and wholesome snack, or use them as a topping for oatmeal, yogurt, or desserts. Enjoy!

These air-fried cinnamon apple chips are crispy, sweet, and packed with flavor. They're a healthier alternative to store-bought chips and make a perfect snack for any time of day. Feel free to adjust the amount of cinnamon and sugar to suit your taste preferences, or omit the sugar entirely for a naturally sweet treat.

Air Fryer Chicken Shawarma

Ingredients:

- 1 lb boneless, skinless chicken thighs, thinly sliced
- 2 tablespoons olive oil
- 2 tablespoons lemon juice
- 2 cloves garlic, minced
- 1 teaspoon ground cumin
- 1 teaspoon ground paprika
- 1 teaspoon ground turmeric
- 1/2 teaspoon ground coriander
- 1/2 teaspoon ground cinnamon
- 1/4 teaspoon cayenne pepper (optional, for extra heat)
- Salt and pepper, to taste
- Cooking spray

Instructions:

1. Prepare the Chicken: In a mixing bowl, combine the olive oil, lemon juice, minced garlic, ground cumin, ground paprika, ground turmeric, ground coriander, ground cinnamon, cayenne pepper (if using), salt, and pepper. Mix well to form a marinade. Add the thinly sliced chicken thighs to the bowl and toss until they are evenly coated with the marinade. Cover the bowl and refrigerate for at least 1 hour, or overnight for best results.
2. Preheat the Air Fryer: Preheat your air fryer to 375°F (190°C) for 5 minutes.
3. Arrange in the Air Fryer: Lightly grease the air fryer basket with cooking spray. Arrange the marinated chicken thighs in a single layer in the air fryer basket, making sure they are not touching each other.
4. Air Fry the Chicken: Air fry the chicken thighs at 375°F (190°C) for 12-15 minutes, flipping halfway through the cooking time, until they are cooked through and golden brown on the outside.
5. Serve: Once cooked, remove the chicken shawarma from the air fryer and let it rest for a few minutes before serving.
6. Enjoy: Serve the air fryer chicken shawarma hot as a delicious and flavorful main dish. Enjoy!

This air-fried chicken shawarma is tender, juicy, and packed with Middle Eastern spices. It's perfect for serving with pita bread, hummus, tzatziki sauce, and your favorite salad ingredients for a complete meal. Feel free to customize the seasoning to suit your taste preferences, and adjust the cooking time as needed based on the thickness of the chicken thighs.

Air Fryer Mexican Street Corn

Ingredients:

- 4 ears of fresh corn on the cob, husks removed
- 1/4 cup mayonnaise
- 1/4 cup sour cream or Mexican crema
- 1/4 cup finely chopped cilantro
- 1/2 cup crumbled cotija cheese or feta cheese
- 1 teaspoon chili powder
- 1 lime, cut into wedges
- Salt and pepper, to taste

Instructions:

1. Prepare the Corn: Preheat your air fryer to 400°F (200°C) for 5 minutes. While the air fryer is preheating, carefully remove the husks and silk from the corn on the cob. Rinse the corn under cold water and pat dry with paper towels.
2. Air Fry the Corn: Place the prepared corn on the cob in the preheated air fryer basket in a single layer. Air fry the corn at 400°F (200°C) for 12-15 minutes, flipping halfway through the cooking time, until the corn is tender and lightly charred in spots.
3. Prepare the Toppings: While the corn is cooking, prepare the toppings. In a small bowl, mix together the mayonnaise, sour cream or Mexican crema, and finely chopped cilantro. Crumble the cotija cheese or feta cheese and set aside.
4. Assemble the Mexican Street Corn: Once the corn is cooked, carefully remove it from the air fryer and transfer it to a serving platter. Using a brush or spoon, generously spread the mayonnaise mixture over each ear of corn. Sprinkle the crumbled cheese evenly over the corn, then sprinkle with chili powder. Season with salt and pepper to taste.
5. Serve: Serve the air fryer Mexican street corn immediately with lime wedges on the side for squeezing over the corn.
6. Enjoy: Enjoy the delicious flavors of this classic street food favorite!

This air-fried Mexican street corn is creamy, cheesy, and bursting with flavor. It's the perfect side dish for your next barbecue or Mexican-themed dinner party. Feel free to customize the toppings to suit your taste preferences, such as adding extra chili powder for heat or drizzling with hot sauce.

Air Fryer Spicy Cauliflower Bites

Ingredients:

- 1 head cauliflower, cut into florets
- 1/2 cup all-purpose flour (or chickpea flour for a gluten-free option)
- 1/2 cup water
- 1 teaspoon garlic powder
- 1 teaspoon onion powder
- 1 teaspoon paprika
- 1/2 teaspoon cayenne pepper (adjust to taste for desired spiciness)
- Salt and pepper, to taste
- Cooking spray
- Optional: buffalo sauce or your favorite hot sauce for tossing

Instructions:

1. Prepare the Cauliflower: Preheat your air fryer to 375°F (190°C) for 5 minutes. While the air fryer is preheating, wash the cauliflower and cut it into florets, discarding the stem and leaves.
2. Prepare the Batter: In a mixing bowl, whisk together the all-purpose flour, water, garlic powder, onion powder, paprika, cayenne pepper, salt, and pepper until smooth and well combined. The batter should be thick enough to coat the cauliflower florets.
3. Coat the Cauliflower: Dip each cauliflower floret into the batter, shaking off any excess. Place the coated cauliflower florets on a plate or wire rack to allow any excess batter to drip off.
4. Air Fry the Cauliflower: Lightly grease the air fryer basket with cooking spray. Arrange the coated cauliflower florets in a single layer in the air fryer basket, making sure they are not touching or overlapping.
5. Air Fry: Air fry the cauliflower at 375°F (190°C) for 15-20 minutes, shaking the basket halfway through the cooking time, until the cauliflower is golden brown and crispy on the outside.
6. Optional: Toss with Sauce: If desired, toss the cooked cauliflower bites with buffalo sauce or your favorite hot sauce while they are still warm for extra flavor and spice.
7. Serve: Once cooked, remove the spicy cauliflower bites from the air fryer and serve immediately as a delicious appetizer or snack.

8. Enjoy: Enjoy the spicy cauliflower bites on their own or with your favorite dipping sauce. They're perfect for game day, parties, or as a tasty side dish!

These air-fried spicy cauliflower bites are crispy on the outside, tender on the inside, and packed with flavor. Feel free to adjust the seasonings and spice level to suit your taste preferences, and serve them with ranch dressing, blue cheese dip, or sriracha mayo for dipping.

Air Fryer Caprese Stuffed Chicken

Ingredients:

- 2 boneless, skinless chicken breasts
- 4 slices fresh mozzarella cheese
- 2 slices ripe tomato
- 4 fresh basil leaves
- Salt and pepper, to taste
- 1 tablespoon olive oil
- 1 teaspoon Italian seasoning
- Balsamic glaze, for serving (optional)

Instructions:

1. Prepare the Chicken: Preheat your air fryer to 375°F (190°C) for 5 minutes. While the air fryer is preheating, use a sharp knife to butterfly each chicken breast, creating a pocket for the stuffing. Be careful not to cut all the way through.
2. Stuff the Chicken: Season the inside of each chicken breast with salt and pepper to taste. Place 2 slices of fresh mozzarella cheese, 1 slice of tomato, and 2 fresh basil leaves inside each chicken breast, dividing the ingredients evenly between the two.
3. Secure the Chicken: Use toothpicks to secure the edges of the chicken breasts and hold the stuffing in place.
4. Season the Chicken: Brush the outside of each stuffed chicken breast with olive oil and sprinkle with Italian seasoning, salt, and pepper.
5. Air Fry the Chicken: Lightly grease the air fryer basket with cooking spray. Place the stuffed chicken breasts in the air fryer basket in a single layer, leaving space between them.
6. Air Fry: Air fry the chicken at 375°F (190°C) for 20-25 minutes, flipping halfway through the cooking time, until the chicken is cooked through and the outside is golden brown and crispy.
7. Serve: Once cooked, remove the stuffed chicken breasts from the air fryer and let them rest for a few minutes before serving.
8. Drizzle with Balsamic Glaze: If desired, drizzle the stuffed chicken breasts with balsamic glaze before serving for extra flavor.
9. Enjoy: Serve the air fryer Caprese stuffed chicken hot as a delicious and elegant main dish. Enjoy!

This air-fried Caprese stuffed chicken is juicy, flavorful, and filled with the classic combination of mozzarella cheese, tomato, and basil. It's perfect for serving with a side salad or roasted vegetables for a complete meal. Feel free to customize the stuffing with your favorite ingredients, such as sun-dried tomatoes or pesto, for a delicious twist on this classic dish.

Air Fryer Curried Chickpeas

Ingredients:

- 1 can (15 oz) chickpeas (garbanzo beans), drained and rinsed
- 1 tablespoon olive oil
- 1 teaspoon curry powder
- 1/2 teaspoon ground cumin
- 1/2 teaspoon ground coriander
- 1/4 teaspoon turmeric
- 1/4 teaspoon paprika
- 1/4 teaspoon garlic powder
- 1/4 teaspoon onion powder
- Salt, to taste

Instructions:

1. Prepare the Chickpeas: Rinse the chickpeas under cold water and pat them dry with paper towels. Remove any loose skins by gently rubbing the chickpeas between your fingers.
2. Season the Chickpeas: In a mixing bowl, combine the chickpeas with olive oil, curry powder, ground cumin, ground coriander, turmeric, paprika, garlic powder, onion powder, and salt. Toss until the chickpeas are evenly coated with the seasoning mixture.
3. Preheat the Air Fryer: Preheat your air fryer to 400°F (200°C) for 5 minutes.
4. Air Fry the Chickpeas: Lightly grease the air fryer basket with cooking spray. Spread the seasoned chickpeas in a single layer in the air fryer basket.
5. Air Fry: Air fry the chickpeas at 400°F (200°C) for 15-20 minutes, shaking the basket halfway through the cooking time, until the chickpeas are golden brown and crispy.
6. Serve: Once cooked, remove the curried chickpeas from the air fryer and let them cool for a few minutes before serving.
7. Enjoy: Serve the air fryer curried chickpeas as a crunchy and flavorful snack or appetizer. Enjoy!

These air-fried curried chickpeas are crispy on the outside and tender on the inside, with a delicious blend of spices. They're perfect for snacking on their own or adding to salads, soups, or grain bowls for extra flavor and crunch. Feel free to adjust the seasoning to suit your taste preferences, adding more or less curry powder or other spices as desired.

Air Fryer Chili-Lime Chicken Drumsticks

Ingredients:

- 6 chicken drumsticks
- 2 tablespoons olive oil
- Zest and juice of 1 lime
- 2 cloves garlic, minced
- 1 teaspoon chili powder
- 1/2 teaspoon paprika
- 1/2 teaspoon cumin
- 1/4 teaspoon cayenne pepper (adjust to taste)
- Salt and pepper, to taste
- Fresh cilantro, chopped (for garnish, optional)
- Lime wedges, for serving

Instructions:

1. Prepare the Chicken Drumsticks: Pat the chicken drumsticks dry with paper towels. Score the chicken drumsticks by making shallow cuts across the surface of the skin. This will help the marinade penetrate the meat.
2. Prepare the Marinade: In a mixing bowl, combine the olive oil, lime zest, lime juice, minced garlic, chili powder, paprika, cumin, cayenne pepper, salt, and pepper. Mix well to combine.
3. Marinate the Chicken: Place the chicken drumsticks in a large resealable plastic bag or shallow dish. Pour the marinade over the chicken, making sure to coat each drumstick evenly. Seal the bag or cover the dish and refrigerate for at least 1 hour, or overnight for best results.
4. Preheat the Air Fryer: Preheat your air fryer to 375°F (190°C) for 5 minutes.
5. Air Fry the Chicken Drumsticks: Lightly grease the air fryer basket with cooking spray. Arrange the marinated chicken drumsticks in the air fryer basket in a single layer, making sure they are not touching each other. You may need to cook them in batches depending on the size of your air fryer.
6. Air Fry: Air fry the chicken drumsticks at 375°F (190°C) for 25-30 minutes, flipping halfway through the cooking time, until the chicken is golden brown and cooked through. The internal temperature of the chicken should reach 165°F (74°C).
7. Serve: Once cooked, remove the chili-lime chicken drumsticks from the air fryer and transfer them to a serving platter. Garnish with chopped cilantro, if desired, and serve with lime wedges on the side for squeezing over the chicken.

8. Enjoy: Serve the air fryer chili-lime chicken drumsticks hot as a delicious and flavorful main dish. Enjoy!

These air-fried chili-lime chicken drumsticks are juicy, tender, and packed with zesty flavor. They're perfect for serving with rice, roasted vegetables, or a fresh salad for a complete meal. Adjust the amount of cayenne pepper to suit your desired level of spiciness, and feel free to customize the seasoning to your taste preferences.

Air Fryer Mediterranean Veggie Skewers

Ingredients:

- 1 zucchini, sliced into rounds
- 1 yellow squash, sliced into rounds
- 1 red bell pepper, cut into chunks
- 1 yellow bell pepper, cut into chunks
- 1 red onion, cut into chunks
- 8-10 cherry tomatoes
- 2 tablespoons olive oil
- 2 cloves garlic, minced
- 1 teaspoon dried oregano
- 1 teaspoon dried basil
- 1 teaspoon dried thyme
- Salt and pepper, to taste
- Wooden skewers, soaked in water for 30 minutes

Instructions:

1. Prepare the Vegetables: Preheat your air fryer to 375°F (190°C) for 5 minutes. While the air fryer is preheating, prepare the vegetables by slicing the zucchini and yellow squash into rounds, cutting the bell peppers and red onion into chunks, and keeping the cherry tomatoes whole.
2. Season the Vegetables: In a large mixing bowl, combine the olive oil, minced garlic, dried oregano, dried basil, dried thyme, salt, and pepper. Add the prepared vegetables to the bowl and toss until they are evenly coated with the seasoning mixture.
3. Assemble the Skewers: Thread the seasoned vegetables onto the soaked wooden skewers, alternating the different vegetables to create colorful skewers.
4. Air Fry the Skewers: Lightly grease the air fryer basket with cooking spray. Place the assembled veggie skewers in the air fryer basket in a single layer, making sure they are not touching each other.
5. Air Fry: Air fry the Mediterranean veggie skewers at 375°F (190°C) for 10-12 minutes, flipping halfway through the cooking time, until the vegetables are tender and slightly charred.
6. Serve: Once cooked, remove the veggie skewers from the air fryer and transfer them to a serving platter.

7. Enjoy: Serve the air fryer Mediterranean veggie skewers hot as a delicious and nutritious side dish or appetizer. Enjoy!

These air-fried Mediterranean veggie skewers are packed with flavor and make a colorful addition to any meal. They're perfect for serving alongside grilled meats, fish, or tofu, or as a standalone vegetarian dish. Feel free to customize the vegetables and seasoning to suit your taste preferences, and serve them with your favorite dipping sauce or tzatziki for extra flavor.

www.ingramcontent.com/pod-product-compliance
Lightning Source LLC
LaVergne TN
LVHW062048070526
838201LV00080B/2196